Lydia Ann Davis Merrill

LIFE OF A PIONEER GIRL

Family History StoryBooks

Long ago, in the lush, green lands of Ontario, Canada, lived a little girl named Lydia Ann Davis. She was the youngest member of the family, which included a mother and father, Sarah Ann and Isaac, and eight older brothers and sisters who all loved her very much. Every day was an adventure for curious Lydia. She loved trying new things and worked hard learning to ride horses, catch fish, sew, quilt, and cord wool.

While Lydia was still very young, missionaries came to her town, sharing stories about a new church called the Church of Jesus Christ of Latter-day Saints. Her family was captivated by the Spirit they felt confirming the truth that God had called a prophet to restore His gospel to the Earth.

In 1840, when Lydia was 7 years old, her family decided to move all the way to Nauvoo, Illinois where they could be closer to other members of the Church. They packed their belongings and said goodbye to their beautiful Canadian home. For more than 800 miles, little Lydia rode in a wagon pulled by horses along bumpy roads and trails.

Nauvoo was a bustling community of hope and hard work for the Saints. Driven by a spirit of cooperation and faith, Lydia and her family helped build homes, shops, and farms. Under the guidance of the prophet, Joseph Smith, the Saints also laid the foundations for the Nauvoo Temple. Life in Nauvoo was marked by a strong commitment to serve the Lord, despite the pressures and prosecution they faced from other people.

There were many people who did not understand why families like Lydia's would change their lives and sacrifice so much to follow Joseph Smith. They did not understand that God was leading and teaching the Saints. It made those people angry. Sometimes the angry people would come to Nauvoo to start fights, hurt people, and even burn down shops and homes. Living in Nauvoo became scary. Even though she was scared, Lydia believed that Heavenly Father would take care of her and her family.

One day, news came that Joseph Smith had been killed by the angry mob of people. Lydia saw the grief and fear that spread through her family and fellow Saints. They felt vulnerable about the future. Who was going to lead the Church now? How much longer could they stay in Nauvoo? Where else could they go?

In 1846, Lydia and her family packed their bags once again. The new Prophet, Brigham Young, had received instructions from God to move the Saints west so they could live more peacefully. It was the middle of winter and Lydia was just 13 years old when she crossed the cold Mississippi River and traveled into untamed territory with her family.

After about 200 miles, they came to a settlement called Mount Pisgah in Iowa. The Saints there had run out of supplies and desperately needed help. Lydia was inspired by her father, Isaac, when he jumped into action to help those who were in need even though he was tired and hungry from his own journey. Isaac went with another man to obtain food and provisions for the hungry Saints. Lydia watched her father leave with mixed feelings of hope and gratitude, as well as fear for his safety.

Isaac and his friend were able to collect all the food and materials they needed and were soon on their way back to their families. On the last leg of their journey though, they had to cross a river. When they had left Mount Pisgah, the river crossing had been easily manageable. This time, however, melting snow had filled the river and it was flowing much faster and higher than before.

Weighed down with all the provisions they had collected, Isaac and his companion attempted to cross the swollen river separating them from their families and friends. The raging river overpowered their wagon and swept the horses, both men, and their cargo away. Isaac was washed away by the forceful currents, and was lost to the river.

Heart-ache consumed Lydia. She was devastated by the loss of her father and her heart broke again every time she saw her mother and siblings mourning. Despite losing Isaac, her mother, Sarah, still had firm faith in the Lord and knew she needed to finish the trek West with her family. Lydia did everything she could to be a support and a help to her mother.

In 1850 the family spent nearly five months traveling with wagons and horses, and all their belongings across prairies, forests, and even through mountains. At times they endured blistering heat with no way to cool off or the biting cold with only a few thin blankets to go around. At the end of the long and dangerous trail, they finally arrived in the Salt Lake Valley.

In her new home Lydia received her patriarchal blessing—a message from God just for her—telling her about her spiritual gifts and the wonderful things she could do in her life. This blessing was like a warm, comforting blanket, giving Lydia strength and confidence as she embraced her new life in Utah.

Lydia spent her time working for other families by helping with household chores and using skills like sewing that her mother had taught her. During her time as a seamstress, Lydia met a wonderful man named Laban Morrill. They became close friends and began to fall in love.

In 1854 Lydia Ann Davis and Laban Morrill were married in a big, beautiful building called the Council House. Lydia was excited to start her family with Laban, hoping for many days filled with love and laughter.

Just a few years later, Lydia made a special trip to the Endowment House. There, she made covenants with God in sacred ceremonies that deepened her faith and commitment to her Heavenly Father. Lydia felt peace knowing she was part of a community that shared her beliefs and supported each other through life's challenges.

Later that year, a tragedy happened. Some strangers came traveling through the area on their way to California and weren't very kind to the communities they passed through. The communities, in turn, became angry with the travelers. The anger and hostility on both sides escalated until finally a huge fight broke out and many people were hurt or killed. This disaster that became known as the Mountain Meadows Massacre.

Lydia was worried for her husband, Laban, who had gone to try and help. He had traveled up to Salt Lake City to tell Brigham Young what was going on, but by the time Brigham's instruction to let the travelers go made it back to Southern Utah, it was too late. As news came in about the massacre, Lydia prayed for her husband to come home safely. The Lord answered her prayers and Laban was soon able to return to her.

Lydia's heart learned new kinds of joy and sorrow as she welcomed her first two babies into the world. Both of them were boys but neither one lived for long. Through her tears, Lydia found strength by relying on the Savior as well as her family and community, who gathered around her with love and support.

In 1858, Lydia had another baby boy named Alexander. This time, joy stayed in Lydia's home as little Alexander grew. Before long she had eight beautiful children to love and care for. Lydia treasured being a mother and cherished her time with her children, teaching them all about the beautiful world around them and the joy she found in the Gospel of Jesus Christ.

Years later, Lydia and her family moved to a place called Iron County to help build a new community. It was hard work, but Lydia knew how to be strong. She helped plant crops and build houses, always hoping to make a better world for her children.

They settled many towns in the county, including Johnson's Fort (Enoch), Junction, Virgin, and Summit. Some of those towns still exist today, and others no longer have inhabitants.

In 1885, a new law changed things for Lydia's family. Laban was taken to court because he had more than one wife, which was now against the law. It was a scary time, but the judge decided to be kind and let Laban come back home. Lydia was relieved and grateful.

After many years and many changes, Lydia and Laban had to make a hard decision. They decided to live apart from each other in order to follow the new laws. It was a sad time for Lydia, but she knew it was important to obey the rules and keep her family safe. Laban still visited Lydia often and continued to refer to her as his wife even though they had moved apart.

One day, while visiting Lydia, Laban's other wife, Permelia, fell from the wagon they were riding in and got very hurt. Lydia helped take care of her, showing her kindness and love, even during tough times. Despite every effort to nurse her back to health, Permelia passed away. Lydia and Permelia had been close friends and she was greatly missed by both Laban and Lydia.

On a quiet day in September 1893, Lydia passed away. Her life was a testament of resilience and faith. She embraced her roles as a wife, mother, and disciple of Christ. Even though she had to face many sorrows and heart-aches, her faith in the Lord never wavered and that enabled her to be strengthened by her experiences.

Lydia's life was not just about survival but about making a meaningful impact—a legacy of strength and love for her children and her community, echoing the teachings and tenacity that had been hallmarks of her entire life journey. Her story is remembered and cherished, teaching her descendants about courage, love, and perseverance.

Lydia Ann Davis Morrill

LIFE OF A PIONEER GIRL

OCTOBER 19, 1833 - SEPTEMBER 22, 1893

My Relationship:

FamilySearch.org ID: KWNV-65N

Book Created for Lydia's Great-Great Granddaughter,
Jennifer Huntington

Order More Copies at familyhistorystorybooks.com

Family History StoryBooks

Did You Like this Book?
Let us tell YOUR story!
Come visit us at familyhistorystorybooks.com and
we can turn your own treasured stories into a
children's book

SCAN
ME

Lydia Ann Davis Morrill

Laban Morrill

Council House - Salt Lake City, Utah

**Lydia's Headstone
Junction, Utah**

**Lydia's Home
Near Junction, Utah**

Made in the USA
Las Vegas, NV
10 October 2024

96633824R00019